Angus the G

Written and Illustrated by Michelle Roche

For Clara,
who has yet to realize
that siblings are generally the same species.

Most dogs like to bark.

They “woof”
at squirrels.

They "arf" at
the mailman.

They sadly howl,
"bow wow wow wow wow"
when their dinner is late.

We rely on barking dogs to tell us when something is amiss.

Angus was a
very large dog
who never
barked at
anything.

He silently watched while the bunnies played in the garden, eating all of Dad's vegetables.

He silently
watched the
delivery man
bring
packages up
the steps.

He silently watched a bicycle club ride past the house. Every other dog on the street barked at the bicycles...

but not Angus.

Angus wouldn't even bark when he needed to go outside. Mom had to hang bells on the door so he could ring them with his nose.

And in the
middle of the
night,

if his blanket
fell off,

he walked over
to Mom and
silently stared
at her until she
woke up and
tucked him
back in.

One quiet afternoon, Mom was reading a book, the baby was napping, and Angus was walking around the house looking for the perfect sun spot.

All of a sudden,
Mom heard a
"rrrrrrrrrruffff"
come from the dining
room.

It couldn't be...

"rrrruffffff!"
"rrrrrrrruffff!"

"ruff ruff ruff ruff!"

Mom was quite surprised and very worried.
"I'm coming Angus, what is it?"

He was at the window barking with his hackles up!

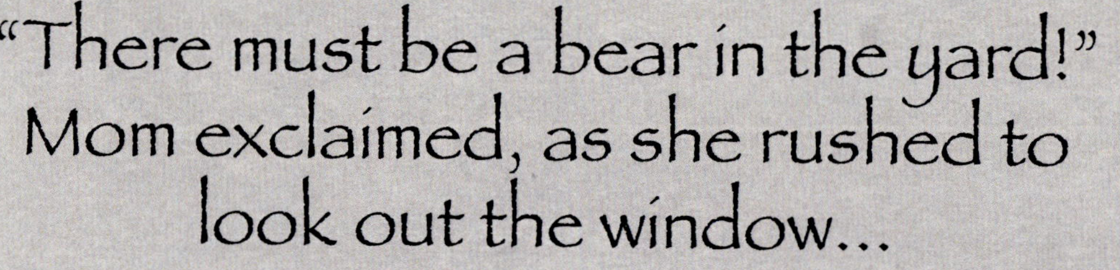

"There must be a bear in the yard!" Mom exclaimed, as she rushed to look out the window...

...but when she scanned the yard she saw nothing at all!

"Perhaps there is someone walking on the trail?" Mom looked towards the woods but she still couldn't see anything.

"Maybe a man has come to read the meter?"

This time Mom opened the window and stuck her head way out, so she could look down close to the house.

No one was there!

Mom was confused.

She pulled her head back in,
and looked down to Angus.

“What’s wrong, Angus?”

“Nothing has ever bothered you before.
What is it that has finally made you bark?”

Angus put his nose down to the bottom of the window and gave another determined, "ruff ruff rrrrruff!"

And there,

on the window sill,

Mom finally found it.

Creeping along the
edge was the
teeniest
little ladybug
she had ever seen.

"You CAN'T be serious,"
Mom said, as she laughed out loud.

But
Angus
bounced
on his paws,

and flapped his ears,

and gave the bug a big,
disgusted
snort.

The ladybug finally flew out the open window, and Angus was relieved to watch her go.

He stood by the window until she was out of sight.

Then Angus walked over to his sun spot,
circled until the sun shone right on his nose,
and flopped down for his nap.

BEWARE
OF
DOG

Michelle is a veterinarian with a lifelong love of dogs and art. Angus is a Rhodesian Ridgeback with multiple titles in obedience and agility. He enjoys time in the spotlight as a canine model and time in the sunlight as a lazy porch dog.

(And when his ego gets the best of him, Michelle just finds a ladybug to put him in his place.)

Made in the USA
San Bernardino, CA
05 December 2017